give me your hand

– pablo neruda

the mischief café

poetry at home with toast (buttered!) & tea

t.s. poetry press

𝑡𝑠 T. S. Poetry Press • New York

T. S. Poetry Press
Ossining, New York
Tspoetry.com

© 2014 by T. S. Poetry Press

All rights reserved.

This book contains poems from T. S. Poetry Press titles. Used with permission of T. S. Poetry Press. Haikubes, mentioned in the poem "Haikubes" is a game from Chronicle Books.

Cover image by L.L. Barkat. llbarkat.com

ISBN 978-0-9898542-5-2

for our poetry baristas
who generously pour the joy of virtual coffee & tea

Donna, Elizabeth, Sandra,
thank you for loving our community

and for all those who support poetry
with us every day

it wouldn't be the same without you

About The Mischief Café

At *Tweetspeak Poetry*, it has been our delight to bring poetry to people, right where they are. To bring together established poets and poets taking first steps. And to invite those who thought they could *never* be a part of poetry to dip in without fear. Because we strongly believe poetry is for life. Not for ivory towers.

Somewhere along the way, as part of our poetry merry-making, we opened The Mischief Café. It's a "welcome" space on our website. But also somewhere along the line, it began to feel like more.

*Maybe The Mischief Café should not just be **virtual**,* we started to think. And so it began. The idea of a traveling café, bringing poetry to people right where they are. In their own homes, amidst friends. With toast (buttered) and tea.

It's an idea that's still working itself out, but for now, sometimes a member of our *Tweetspeak Poetry* team will come to tea with poetry. And sometimes poetry lovers won't want to wait for that. So they'll make a little poetry mischief on their own.

How to Make Your Own Mischief Café

We first introduced the idea of a traveling Mischief Café in a Saturday morning conversation on social media. We promised to sometimes show up for poetry and tea. The idea was simple: tea, toast, poems.

By mid-morning in the conversation, it became clear that each host or hostess would have unique ideas and that there would be no "one way" to run a Mischief Café.

Besides *reading* poetry, some people wanted to *write* collaborative poetry. Others wanted to include poetry games. One decided a café menu might be in order. No doubt, some were in it for the cinnamon toast. But many agreed it would be nice to have something people could keep from the gathering. Maybe a journal type book in which a communal poem was started. Or maybe something more like a guest book, in which people could write their favorite lines from their time together, or simply sign their names.

So, depending on what kind of host, hostess, or invited guest you'd like to be, consider this to be a guide, a journal, or a guest book you keep over time (you're going to want to host or attend more than one Mischief Café, we suspect).

Read the poems from these pages, aloud at the café. Or make your own poetry fun, with titles you pick for the gathering, by theme or by poet. Trace everyone's hands into the book, or add photos and art. Pen poems together, or make memories with borrowed lines you put under one of the provided poem titles (Did you know that borrowing lines from established poems and making them into a new poem is an age-old method that comes from the Greeks? This kind of poem is called a *cento*.)

Do what you like. It's your poetry life. It's your café.

Our café motto has been, *magic, mischief, merriment, and mirth*. We hope you find a little of that in these pages, or pour it in over time. We also hope you become the happiest poetry hosts and hostesses (or attendees) the world has ever seen.

Toast with your tea?

What's in the Book

Poems. Of course. Possible poem titles (you'll know these by the way they sit in bold, alone and waiting, at the top of a page). And, speaking of pages, you'll find these, blank—to make your poetry café way with collaborative poems, art, or cento poems on themes of your own choosing.

Read poems, or make poems, take pictures of your times together. Share them with us for an album we'll make online.

Let's make poetry mischief!

You can find us at tweetspeakpoetry.com
or tweet us @tspoetry

Tell me a poem, a story
of a favored poet or poem,
one who changed your life,
your mind, opened up
possibilities, or made you
feel secure as your anchors,
your moorings, were removed.
Speak to me of your need;
describe the expectations
(are they great ones?), explain
how we soar together, toward
the sun, if not the moon,
tell me how I become

part of your larger self.

—Glynn Young

You Know It's a Threshold When

T. S. Poetry Press • 11

If You Want to See

My House

    walls stand
close to hold
the chill at bay
like children do,
huddled in grass
fields waiting
for the school bell.

—David K. Wheeler

And some days all she wants to be
is a county road arcing away from electricity, past
fallow hay fields, on the brink of the blind curve.

—Anne M. Doe Overstreet, from "Edges"

The Tragic Hero

I Choose

Li Po

1

Li Po knew
the fecund trees
full of blossoms,
the tea bushes
flush with leaves,
sweet scent rising
from snow-petaled earth,
spears rolled—or broken—
between fingers and thumb

2

Every morning
I am Li Po,
if only I hear
the expectant cup

3

And if the porcelain overturns,
what then?

4

the snow-petaled earth
the snow-petaled earth

—L.L. Barkat, in *How to Read a Poem*

Sore Chasing Dreams

Sore with chasing
dreams, I scatter

fresh-bought seed
in un-neat rows.

Ravens, wheeling
through cotton-balled clouds,

show me the meaning
of passion

at ground level.

—Maureen E. Doallas

Edges

How to Write a Poem

T. S. Poetry Press • 25

Resolutions

Wear nonsensical heels   investigate the suspicion of doubt   spend more time gathering stones   date a baker and learn to taste the difference in flours   impress vermilion upon a lip   emulate spiders: touch everything first before engaging   ask to be called Jane   collect Janes   paint the bathroom black   memorize a Basho poem that is not about leaving   call your mother only when half-drunk   have an icon of Teresa of Avila beside you when you call   study walls, what they keep in   eat some animal you've never seen   draw what that animal tastes like   clean out the deep freeze in the basement   call your mother Elizabeth as if by mistake   attend a Beekeepers of America meeting   read a biography about Amelia Earhart   change the cat's name to Amelia   dream of Icarus   pray beneath low ceilings. Maybe then.

—Anne M. Doe Overstreet

Boss

Stares at the corner where
two glass walls meet, almost
the exact point where the sun
sets, caught in the rise
of his people asking, probing
how and more and the descent
of his own boss seeking cuts.
He chooses the way
he's been taught, looking
upward, knowing there's little
reward in the daily, where
life is.

—Glynn Young

Home Is

Alone, I

How to Run a Mischief Café

One vision
involves a formal beginning.

                              Heightened attention.

Silence.

                              Very little spoken, if at all.

                To the point of shared awkwardness.

Hear the knife scrape against the toast,
the teacup slip into its saucer.
Only hands speak.
Once ears have become butterfly nets,
the poems visit.
Nets can be placed in notebooks.

But then comes Act Two.
Releasing the butterflies.
Voices. Sharing.
Now comes the louder, livelier play.

  —Matthew Kreider, from the Saturday social media conversation

The Backwoods

There the fiddleheads reach
upward. Air ambles
in fog and pollen and
imprints left around
the roots of giant pines.
They call you
back, if you're listening:
moans, grunts, or wails,
like something roams
between the trees and
leaves tufts of hair for us
to find and follow back,
far into the forest.
The stories go further back.

—David K. Wheeler

Coming of Age

Introduction to Poetry

Petit à Petit L'Oiseau Fait Son Nid

Little by little, they say,
the bird makes its nest.
I have been making mine
in silvered hemlocks, time
after time; today I used a red
thread I found near the garden.

I used to dream of living in a garden,
listening to words white orchids say
to emerald hummingbirds, red-
throated, stealing gold for nests
the size of women's thimbles, time
beating between breaths, a rhythm mine

could never find trapped, as in a mine
long hollowed, tapped black garden
that metamorphosed over time,
caught sounds of earth-on-earth say,
Come bed yourself on rock-hard nest,
turn death to sapphire, diamond, ruby red.

Rumor spreads: inside the earth is red,
molten, thrusting gold like mine
into the sun, into evening's nest
that sits above an empty garden
where orchids do not say
it is time

it is time
to ravel rays from ravished dreams, red
and unremembered; it is time to say
what is yours and what is mine
it is time to turn the garden
into earth, find fool's gold for a nest.

I have been making such a nest,
little by little, time after time,
I have been dreaming near a garden
in threads of memories, ruby red.
I have been claiming what is mine
and inviting you to say

you want the nest, the gold turning red,
the time we knew was mine,
the garden waiting, for what you have to say.

—L.L. Barkat, in *How to Read a Poem*

(This poem is a form called the *sestina*. There are two more in the book, if you'd like to go on a poetry treasure hunt to find them. You can read more about sestinas at tweetspeakpoetry.com.)

And Still I Dream

Tell Me a Poem

pnw. pacific.north.west.

we are

so far away

that to make it worth your while,
it really ought to be a weekend tea—
not to be confused with weakened tea,

of course.

sister/brotherhood
of the traveling teapots.

—Darlene S., from the Saturday social media conversation

Is it possible
to make small poetry cubes
and pile them in sugar bowls
and you must
scoop them out with a spoon?

—Sandra Heska King, from the Saturday social media conversation

When You Are Old

It's Like This, I Remember

But

I will   insist
on coffee.

—Karen Swallow Prior, from the Saturday social media conversation

Haikubes

And another reason
to come to Little Rock:

I have these.

—Laura Lynn Brown, from the Saturday social media conversation

Give Me Your Hand

How to Read a Poem

After a Poem by David K. Wheeler

The silence goes further back.
I thought of that today. It was the way
we were told to be seen and not heard,
and pinched if we transgressed at the table.
It was the way he slept in the living room by night
and looked through us by day, as if we didn't exist,
as if we made   no sound   at all.

—L.L. Barkat, in *Love, Etc.*

Leda

My sister tells a story about a swan and a jeweled strand.
I have never thought of myself as a bird before.
A heron stabs after the half moon among the current,
then lifts off, carving into the horizon.
The sea shirs the sand where my foot rests.
Caught in the mirror, her daughter blooms pale,
hung from the morning like a pearl pendant.

—Anne M. Doe Overstreet

Maslow's Hierarchy

My Real Name

On Restlessness

I've been asking myself the same question.
I know you think you want to know everything;
I would like to understand how we operate.
But I'm afraid we've both been losing sleep.
Come morning, we'll step onto the floor
with no more than a yawn, stretch, or a blink.

I won't have the time it takes to blink
before today has again stifled any question
that might hinder my progress across the floor.
And now you think that I know everything,
for the nights I spent your waking hours asleep.
This is simply the only way I can operate.

Suppose revolutions weren't how days operate.
Suppose we relied on how often we blink
to decide the time between waking and sleep.
I don't think we would have any question
about the sun, zoology, God, and everything.
We'll spend hours charting stars, backs to the floor.

When you can make angels touch the floor,
there will be nothing left to manually operate.
The universe will be in control of everything,
assuring us of this when we watch the stars blink.
What makes us anxious will be out of the question;
what has kept us up will sing us back to sleep.

Until we find answers, let's at least try to sleep.
Pull your blankets back to your bed from the floor.
If it helps, find some paper: write your question.
Mine merely asks *How do you and I operate?*
I wrote it when my hands were numb, I couldn't blink,
and I was nervous for the state of everything.

There was never a time that I knew everything.
There wasn't a night I wanted you to lose sleep.
There are some words you can say with a blink.
There are nights I wake up curled on the floor.
There are appliances that refuse to operate.
There are solutions that don't have a question.

Today you woke with everything tossed across the floor,
from elbows thrown in your sleep—the ways you operate
that make you blink, like you answered your own question.

—David K. Wheeler

I've Been Asking

Baby,

Spring Dress

I love the unknown in you,
the unfair, the shy backs of your knees,
the colony of dimples
that sleep in moon-shaped huts

leaning

toward your mouth.

—Dave Malone

Immolation

As the horizon looms, flips over to present
an endless span of waves, I give up, surrender.
My fate's the fate of falling. I guess I hoped for recognition,
that when I pushed my arms into the hostile sun
he would look up and see my face, the frame
of limb so like his lover, perhaps invoke my name.

I imagine women fainting at the thought
of this lovely form's ravagement, the taint
of char hot enough to warp a wooden strut,
melt wax, and singe. But Daedelus flies on.
The body will soften momentarily, pliable if heavy,
finding shape hours later, so I devise my final self.

The scent surely travels downwind
in the contrail of smoke he, at least, could see.
I thought he'd catch me; if nothing else
to save the contraption with its maze
of gears and levered joints. I counted on,
I understood, he loved the thing.

—Anne M. Doe Overstreet

Resolutions

The Long Journey

A Feeling Grew Into a Hope

A feeling grew
into a hope.

It started out
a worry whorled

the way a conch
flips and turns

until out
goes inside

and deep
hard-shelled

feeling becomes invisible.

Out of warm waters
ocean's pink-lipped horn

trumpeted the sound
of tears evaporating

in motions chiming
to the heart's recovery.

—Maureen E. Doallas

The Tale of Genji: Abridged, by

Murasaki
was not her real name.

*

Did you know that *Murasaki*
means purple?

*

When they bound up Genji's boyish hair,
the cord they used was

*

Did you know (how could you?)
that the first time a reader chose to insult my work, she called it

*

Purple is the color of closeness.
The cord was

*

Murasaki
is her real name.

—L.L. Barkat, in *The Novelist*

A Love Poem Is

My Voice

A Restoration

Ochre bathroom cabinets
sold in sets as if antique
storage space were limited
only by the dust it's kept
years too long. The shelves begin
showing age when cleaned with cloth
doused in polish, oil, or stain.
Slats, untouched for decades, weep,
sagging under all the strain
to maintain what age has stripped.

—David K. Wheeler

A light movement of wind,
a small ripple in the water,
a comment, a tweet, a post,
a few words, and it begins.
A storm, a tsunami,
a hurricane, an eruption
sudden and unexpected,
a crash, and it begins.
Back to normal becomes
a place of no return.

—Glynn Young

If Life Was a Drink

T. S. Poetry Press • 83

How Will I Make My Way?

Thunderboomer

April wind batters Ozark afternoon.
Redbuds bleed purple on the lawn.
Gray gnaws all the way down
to toe-stumbling roots.
Lightning forces squirrels into flight.
The house cries dark with hope
as you rise from the breakfast wasteland
we savored like hipbones.
I follow you into the bedroom
where you curl against me,
the gale smacking then cupping
the front door into giving up.
You are melty as butter.
Clouds blacken outside
like toast.

—Dave Malone

The Pants of Existence

Burn this light my
my, o my—
not in Kansas any less than
this place of fur spangles
dangling on the ankles
of fate like
bells of hells,
transforming the middle ear
to the inner circle of
laughter, where I crease
the pants of existence
and press the life out. If
only the socks matched!

—Marci Rae Johnson & Yvonne Robery, in *How to Read a Poem*

The Right Word Would

To Devise the Self

Sour Plums

A jackhammer cracks apart concrete slabs.
At the bus stop two girls in hoodies gossip loudly,
curse at traffic. They think they can shock us
as we bend beneath the feral plum tree.
We are in the season of blossoms, white swans
silking the backs of our neck,
dappling our dirty shoes. Next month the tree
will begin to form green fists, hard and destined
to become fruit that is barely edible
but will fatten the squirrels, help the rats
through winter. The spastic boy flails by
in his running suit, and I try to love
the sour flesh of our future,
wonder if given enough sugar the plums
would yield some pleasure, bruised surface
bursting in syrup as I search for the right word
to describe the stone heart and the way it insists
on repeating itself every spring.

—Anne M. Doe Overstreet

To the lake, to the ribbon
red, to the time of Kantay,
to the purple shell to the
day of Portlant to the year
of 280 to the place you know
to the people you love, to the
things you think to the places
you dream of, to the light you
seek to what keeps you from
wondering to the love you
give to the love you receive
to what you know is the secret
to the path that you know
is the road to follow.

—Sonia Barkat, age 9, in *Love, Etc.*

This is a poem form called a *catalog* poem. You can read more about catalog poems at tweetspeakpoetry.com.

Spring's Verb Says

Wearing It Would Mean

Sleeping in Grandmother Wolfe's House

Buried here in sheets in this darkened room,
sometimes time sits heavy on the soul.
Some evenings with a last over-the-shudder
look out the window, Red finds herself receding
further, further back, to stone, becoming
the dead thing that fell from the branch,
or the bird-bitten, unplucked callow drupe.

This is the bed where she was born.
The mirror tipped in its walnut frame pins her
flat against the wall, same axe-blade face
suspended there above a crocheted doily
that her grandmother saw, that woman
whose knife pared each portion to its core,
the crevassed heart of apricot and plum.

—Anne M. Doe Overstreet

Whispered

I should tell you
about my hands, small
and experienced.

The other night,
when my youngest daughter
said, as I tucked her into bed,

Tell me something. Tell me anything,
I turned off the light and whispered this:

when I cut the beets tonight,
the red water went all into
the lines on my hands—

so many lines.

—L.L. Barkat, in *Love, Etc.*

Birth Comes

If It Was Quiet

T. S. Poetry Press • 103

Un done

The end of the day does not break, like glass—
maybe; you can catch it, with broken string
on an old piano, *black notes white notes*
falling out the window and the shatter—
bends. Breaks. The other cacophony sits
silently watching, fingers bend like wood

looks on the bench; here the wind through the wood
like broken wind chimes—in a pile of glass—
swallows, noiselessly, the sunrise; and sits.
The whistle doesn't know the sound of string
softly shushing sound asleep, but shatters
silence with faint white *almost-music-notes*

climbing up the wall and through the roof, notes—
sing in a voice like ivory and wood
higher and higher above the shatters
of your glass, *tall slim clear glass*
and at the very top; tips, trips, *falls...* strings
descending, rushing, howling, and—sits.

Upon the ground, other melodies sit
writes out letters in a shaky hand, notes
in brown ink; one by one pulls up the strings
wrestles with song, a savage battle, wood
stained with inky blood—or bloody ink—glass
overturned; lying in pieces, shatters.

And… silence. …*Darkness. Don't look—it shatters
if you look at it too hard* but… here, sits
under the sky; plucking stars, shining glass,
sewing them into a cloak—bejeweled notes
like the firmament itself; they all would
hang like gossamer, silver spider strings.

Test it out for yourself. Wrapped tight with strings,
you strain to pull free; frenzied, soft, shatters
to lie flung across the old stone, old wood
whispers in your ear; tells you, *sit, sit, sit*—
listen to the voice in the wind, the notes
in the old piano, encased in glass.

Carve out a tree from wood, it falls in strings—
push the glass out a window, it shatters—
and when you're tired, sit—hear the last notes.

—Sara Barkat, age 15, in *Love, Etc.*

I Meant to Thank You

Whispered

T. S. Poetry Press • 109

This Has Been a Summer of Moths

As if born the moment
we opened to the dark,
as if they'd been breeding
behind thyme, the tin of Earl Grey,

silver slips rise
from a bed of linen,
from damp-scented woolens.
Drifting out of cupboard doors

unsunned and not called
to any lit flame,
it took a week to determine
a scattered flock

instead of one soft ash
resurrected again and again.
Shivering somnambulists
baffled by glass, they die for lack.

They go to dust
on the windowsill, a wing fading
to a translucent brown sail, prepared
around the absence of body.

—Anne M. Doe Overstreet

Spring Thaw

Heads up:

tiny shoots

break earth's shell

spring up

from winter's

bed of dreams

showing us

how to make

a comeback

every time

—Maureen E. Doallas

Poems Selected From These T. S. Poetry Press Titles

Contingency Plans, by David K. Wheeler
Delicate Machinery Suspended, by Anne M. Doe Overstreet
How to Read a Poem, by Tania Runyan
Love, Etc., by L.L. Barkat
Neruda's Memoirs, by Maureen E. Doallas
Poetry at Work, by Glynn Young
The Novelist, by L.L. Barkat
O: Love Poems from the Ozarks, by Dave Malone

All other poems are "found poems" from the Saturday morning social media conversation. Used with permission. (A "found poem" is a poem you find from someone's words, or on signs, or in movies, etc. You get the idea. You can read more about found poems at tweetspeakpoetry.com.)

Another Great Title for Your Café

How to Read a Poem: Based on the Billy Collins Poem "Introduction to Poetry," by Tania Runyan

No reader, experienced or new to reading poems, will want to miss this winsome and surprising way into the rich, wonderful conversations that poetry makes possible.

—David Wright, Assistant Professor of English at Monmouth College, IL

From the Back Cover of *How to Read a Poem*

How to read a poem. A lot of books want to teach you just that. How is this one different?

Think of it less as an instructional book and more as an invitation. For the reader new to poetry, this guide will open your senses to the combined craft and magic known as "poems." For the well versed, if you will, this book might make you fall in love again.

How to Read a Poem uses images like the mouse, the hive, the switch (from the Billy Collins poem "Introduction to Poetry")—to guide readers into new ways of understanding poems.

T. S. Poetry Press titles are available online in e-book and print editions. Print editions also available through Ingram.

tspoetry.com

www.ingramcontent.com/pod-product-compliance
Lightning Source LLC
Chambersburg PA
CBHW031943070426
42450CB00006BA/780